M. D. Berlitz

German With or Without a Master

M. D. Berlitz

German With or Without a Master

ISBN/EAN: 9783744759380

Printed in Europe, USA, Canada, Australia, Japan

Cover: Foto ©Paul-Georg Meister /pixelio.de

More available books at **www.hansebooks.com**

GERMAN

WITH OR WITHOUT A MASTER

FORMING WITH

Methode Berlitz

A THOROUGH AND EASY COURSE FOR
SELF-INSTRUCTION OR SCHOOLS

GUIDE FOR PREPARING THE LESSONS

BY

M. D. BERLITZ

NEW YORK :

BERLITZ & CO., MADISON SQUARE

PRESS OF
M. J. PENDERGAST, 137 West 23d Street,
NEW YORK.

PREFACE.

This little work is designed to be used together with the „Methode Berlitz," erstes Buch, for the following purposes, the student preparing each lesson with the "Guide" and then reading and reciting the lesson in the "Method" until he is perfectly familiar with every expression :

(1) For self-instruction : the student in such case reads each lesson over several times aloud and then asks himself the questions of the book, answering them.

(2) For reciprocal instruction in clubs or parties of friends, each member alternately taking the role of the teacher, asking the questions and letting the others answer in turn.   This has the advantage over self-instruction in that the ear is more thoroughly drilled in catching the foreign sounds by hearing other people's voices, and that each student will be able, in his turn, to correct some mistakes made by his fellow-students

(3) For schools in which a course in conversation is desired besides the ordinary course in grammar and translation, both courses being followed in this book.

(4) For schools that have large classes or cannot give a great deal of time to German ; as in this book the students find pronunciation and other difficulties thoroughly explained, so that they can do a great deal of work outside of their recitations.

i

The advantages claimed for this method are :

(a) The lessons are mostly based on object-teaching; this results in the student's associating perception directly with the foreign expressions ; he thus is soon able to think in the foreign idiom.

(b) Nearly all of the lessons are in shape of conversation, in order to give continual drill to the student's ear and tongue.

(c) The most useful is always taught first, the student's mind not being encumbered with rules and word forms that he cannot immediately use and will forget again before needing them.

(d) Where rules are to be given, they are illustrated by striking examples, so that even those who are not good grammarians can fully understand them.

(e) The pronunciation of all difficult words or expressions is as carefully transcribed as possible, thus the students need not constantly rely on their teacher and can. if necessary, progress entirely without him.

(f) All idioms or other difficulties are carefully explained in order to emancipate the students from their teacher as much as possible.

By editing this work we, of course, do not at all mean to contradict our opinion, so frequently expressed and defended, that in schools where German is taught by native instructors and where the classes are small, it is far better to avoid all translation and to learn the pronunciation from the teacher   Consequently, such schools we advise to employ not this book, but the regular Berlitz method only. containing no English whatever.

———————

The key to all exercises contained in this book is published separately.   **Price, $0.25**

INTRODUCTION.

~~~~~~

𝕯𝖆𝖘 𝖀𝖑𝖕𝖍𝖆𝖇𝖊𝖙 (dass alfabait') THE ALPHABET.

𝕬 𝖆 a,	𝕭 𝖇 b,	𝕮 𝖈 c,	𝕯 𝖇 d,	𝕰 𝖊 e,
name: ah	bay	tsay	day	ay
𝕱 𝖋 f,	𝕲 𝖌 g,	𝕳 𝖍 h,	𝕴 𝖎 i,	𝕴 𝖏 j,
ef	gay	hah	ee	yot†
𝕶 𝖎 k,	𝕷 𝖑 l,	𝕸 𝖒 m,	𝕹 𝖓 n,	𝕺 𝖔 o,
kah	el	em	en	oh
𝕻 𝖕 p.	𝕼 q q.	𝕽 𝖗 r,	𝕾 𝖋 (𝖘*) s,	𝕿 𝖙 t,
pay	koo	airr	es	tay
𝖀 𝖚 u,	𝖁 𝖛 v,	𝖂 𝖜 w,	𝖃 𝖝 x,	𝖄 𝖞 y,
oo	fow	vay	iks	ip'sillohn
		𝖅 𝖟 z,		
		tset.		

---

* ꞵ is used instead of ſ at the end of a word.
† The o almost like u in but.

Pronunciation of Vowels.

					Transcribed by us with:
a	long	is pronounced as in father			ah
	short	" " "		yacht	a
e	long	" " '.		air	ai
	short	" " "		let	e
	final	" " "		open	ə
i	long	" " ·'		machine	ee
	short	" " "		sister	i
o	long	" " "		role	oh
	short	" " ··		mother	o
u	long	" " '·		rule	oo
	short	" " '·		pull	u

Remarks : As the *e* in a suffix (en, el, er) is almost silent, we shall omit it in our transcription entirely or replace it by an apostrophe.

The difference between a long and a short vowel in German is not nearly so great as in English. We have therefore transcribed with long sounds such short ones as the student would be very likely to mispronounce.

Consonants.

b and *d* are pronounced as in English, but at the end of a word they sound like *p* and *t*.

c before e, i, ä, ö, ü is like *ts*, elsewhere like *k*.

g is as in the English *go*, *get*, but at the end of a word the sound approaches that of *k* or that of the German ch. (In different parts of Germany the pronunciation of *g* varies). Remember that though we transcribe the final *g* with *jh* or *hh* (see "compounds") you may pronounce it like *k*

h at the beginning as in *hand*, elsewhere silent.

j always like *y* in *yes*.

q (always followed by *u*) as in the English *quit*.

s before a vowel somewhat like the English *z* ; *st* and *sp* at the beginning of a syllable sound like *sht, shp ;* elsewhere as in English.

t as in English, but like *ts* before the ending *ion*.

v like *f* (except in foreign words).

w like *v*.

x like *ks*.

y occurs now only in foreign words and is pronounced accordingly.

z like *ts*.

The other consonants (*f, k, l, m, n, p, r*) are pronounced as in English.

COMPOUNDS.

Pronounce: *au* like *ou* in *house*, *ai* and *ei* like *ie* in *pie*, *ie* like *ee*, *eu* and *äu* like *oy* in *boy* (=oi).

Double consonants are pronounced like single ones, *ck* stands for *kk*, *tz* for *zz ;* at the end of a word ſſ is replaced by ß (sz), in the body of a word ß has the hissing s-sound but is preceded by a long vowel whilst ſſ follows a short vowel.

sch is like the English *sh*.

ch has three sounds : 1) beginning a word or followed by *s* belonging to the same syllable the sound of *k*, as : Chor=Kohr (Choir), Chriſt=Krist (Christian), Wachs=Vaks (wax). 2) preceded by *a, o, u, au* it has a strong guttural sound (as in the Scotch *loch*) which we shall represent by *hh*. 3) preceded by e, i, ä. ö, ü or a consonant it has a sound that can be described only as resembling the English *sh*, but whilst the English if a dental sound the German is a palatal one. We shall represent it by *jh*.

Die Umlaute (dee oom'-loutə) MODIFIED VOWELS.

ä sounds like *ai* in *hair.*

ö like the **French** *eu* in *peu.* In English there is no exact equivalent; the nearest to it is the sound of *u* in *burn.* We shall transcribe it with œ.

ü sounds like a thick *ee*, (a French *u*). It is pronounced by opening the mouth but little, with protruding lips (as if you were going to whistle). We shall represent it by *ee.*

ACCENT.

In simple words the stress lies on the principal syllable* except in words taken from foreign languages. In compounds each of the parts has an accent, the first being the strongest (as in the English word "snowball). Where in the lessons the accent of a word cannot easily be determined by the learner, we shall indicate it by the sign ' after the accented syllable, or we shall use the sign —' to represent a long syllable with a heavy accent, — for a secondary or lighter accent, ‿' for a short accentuated syllable, ‿ for a short unaccentuated syllable. The accents of the English words: *rainbow, machine, revelation, coincidence, likelihood* would. therefore, be as follows: —'—, ‿ —', ‿ ‿ —'‿, — ‿' ‿ ‿, —' ‿ —.

CAPITAL LETTERS.

Capital letters are used in German at the beginning of a sentence, also for all nouns and for pronouns of the second person

---

* The principal syllable is generally the one before the last.

Erste Lektion (airstə lekts–yohn') FIRST LESSON.

der Bleiſtift,	(dair blie'–stift)	The lead-pencil.
" Stuhl,	(" shtool)	" chair.
" Tiſch,	(" tish)	" table.
" Ofen,	(" ohf'n)	" stove.
" Boden,	(" bohd'n)	" floor.
" Vorhang,	(" for'–hang)*	" curtain.
die Feder,	(dee faid'r)	" pen.
" Kreide,	(" kriedə)	" chalk.
" Tafel,	(" tahf'l)	" blackboard
" Schachtel,	(" shahht'l)	" box.
" Decke,	(" deckə)	" ceiling.
" Wand,	(" vant)	" wall.
" Thüre,	(" teerə)	" door.
das Buch,	(dass boohh)	" book.
" Lineal,	(" lin–yahl')	" ruler.
" Papier,	(" pappeer ‿—')	" paper.
" Pult,	(" pult)	" desk.
" Fenſter,	(" fenst'r)	" window.
" Tintefaß	(" tin'–təfass)	" inkstand.
Was iſt das ?	(vass ist dass)	what is that ?

* Pronouncing *hang* almost as in *Hong-Kong*.

Ja—Nein,	(yah—nien)	yes—no.
nicht,	(nijht, *almost like* nisht)	not.
sondern,	(zond'rn)	but.
weder—noch,	(vaid'r—nohh)	neither—nor.
u. f. w.=und fo weiter,	(oont zoh vie'tr)	and so forth.

Remarks : In German even inanimate objects may be masculine or feminine and, as the articles, pronouns and adjective-endings are different in different genders, care must be taken to learn well the definite article with each noun so as to know if the noun is masculine, feminine or neuter. The rules for distinguishing the genders by the meaning of the word or by its ending are too complicated to be of any use to a beginner, however, it may be remembered that most of the nouns ending in *e* are feminine, those ending in *en* are masculine.

Farben	(farbən)	COLORS,
schwarz,	(shvarts)	black.
rot,	(roht)	red,
grün	(green)	green.
braun,	(broun)	brown.
weiß,	(viess)	white.
blau,	(blou)	blue.
gelb,	(gelp)	yellow.
grau,	(grou)	gray.

er, (air) he —— fie, (zee) she —— es (ess) it

Remark 2 : The English pronoun *it* must be rendered by he (er) or she (fie) if it refers to a masculine or feminine noun.

Wie ift der Bleiftift?   (vee ist dair blie-stift)

How is the pencil.   (= of what color is the pencil).

diefer (masc.), diefe (fem.), diefes (neut.)   this.
(deez'r,   deezə,   deezəs)

welcher (masc.), welche (fem.), welches (neut.),   which.
(veljhər,   veljhə,   veljhəs)

Remark 3 : Notice that the endings of the pronouns and articles are r, e, s respectively for masculine, feminine and neuter.

Remark 4 : Adjectives preceding the noun end in *e*.
Das fchwarze Buch, das weiße Papier, die gelbe (gelbə) Feder.

Zweite Lektion (tsvietə) SECOND LESSON.

lang (lank) long,	furz (kurts*) short
breit (briet) broad,	fchmal (shmahl) narrow
groß (grohs) large,	flein (klien) small
dick (dick) thick,	dünn (deenn) thin†

Remark 5 : The comparative of adjectives is formed by adding *er ;* the vowels a, o, u are generally modified in such a case, i. e. länger (laing'r), fürzer (keerts'r), größer (groes'r), etc.

---

* Do not forget that the *u* is pronounced as in *pull*.

† Sounds almost like *din*.

Remark 6 : The superlative is formed by inserting ſt or eſt between the adjective and its ending, as : der-längſte, das kürzeſte, der größte, die breiteſte, etc. ; as a predicate the superlative is generally preceded by am and ends in ſten, as : am größten (grœst'n), am kleinſten, am kürzeſten (keert'səstn), etc.

So groß wie (zoh grohs vee) as large as, länger als (laing'r als) longer than, am kleinſten the shortest.

Dritte Lektion (drittə) THIRD LESSON.

Kleidungsſtücke (klie'doongs-steeckə —'‿ ‿'‿) cloth-ing, der Rock (rock*) the coat, die Weſte (vestə) the vest, das Beinkleid (bien-klied) the trousers, der Hut (hoot) the hat, das Kleid (klied) the dress, der Schuh (shoo) the shoe, das Taſchentuch (tashn-toohh) the handkerchief, die Kravatte (kravat'ə) the necktie, der Kragen (krahg'n) the collar, die Manſchette (manshet'ə) the cuff, der Handſchuh (hant'-shoo) the glove.

NOMINATIVE.	GENITIVE.
Wer (vair) who	Weſſen (vess'n) whose
der Herr (hairr) the gentleman,	des Herrn (dess hairn)
die Frau (frou) the lady,	der Frau
das Fräulein (froilien) the Miss	des Fräuleins

Remark 7: The English possessive or the word *of* (the gentleman's hat, the hat of the gentleman, the lady's dress, the dress of the lady, the young lady's handkerchief, the handkerchief of the young lady) are translated by the genitive case in German : der Hut des Herrn, das Kleid der Frau, das Taſchentuch des Fräuleins.

---

* The o almost like the u in stuck.

Remark 8 : Mr., Mrs , Miss are also translated by Herr, Frau, Fräulein.

Remark 9 : Before a name the s of the genitive Fräuleins is omitted. Miss Müller's book, das Buch des Fräulein Müller.

Mein (mien) my, Ihr (er) your, sein (zien) his, its, ihr (eer) her.— When these pronouns are adjectives of feminine nouns they end in e as : mein Bleistift (masc) but meine Feder (fem.), sein Taschentuch (neut.) but seine Kravatte (fem.)

Vierte Lektion (feertə) FOURTH LESSON.

gehen,	kommen,	stehen,	sitzen,	liegen,	sein.
(gai'n)	(kom'n*)	(shtai'n)	(zits'n)	(leeg'n)	(zien)
to go	to come	to stand	to sit	to lie	to be

ich (ijh) I, Sie (zee) you, hier (heer) here, dort (dorrt) there.

Remark 10 : The infinitives end all in n, the first person of the verbs ends in e (ich gehe I go, ich komm: I come), the second person in en (Sie gehen you go. Sie kommen you come), the third person in t (er geht (gait) he goes, sie kommt (komt) she comes).

ich bin	Sie sind	er, sie, es ist,	Wo
(ijh bin)	(zee zint)	(air, zee, es ist)	(voh)
I am	you are	he, she, it is	where

Was thue ich? What am I doing? or What do I do? (vass tooə ijh).

Was thun Sie? What are you doing ? or What do you do? (vass toon zee).

---

* The o as in the English *come*.

Was thut er? What is he doing? or What does he do?
(vass toot air).

Remark 11: Expressions like: I am going, I do
go, you are coming, he is standing, he does stand, etc.,
can merely be translated as: I go, you come, he
stands, etc.

Fünfte Lektion (feenfte) FIFTH LESSON.

bewegen,	stillhalten,	berühren,	nehmen
(bevaig'n)	(shtill'haltn)	(bereer'n)	(naim'n)
to move	to hold still	to touch	to take

aufmachen,	zumachen,	hinlegen,	hinstellen
(auf'mahhən)	(tsoo'mahhən)	(hin'laig'n)	(hin'shtell'n)
to open	to close	to lay down	to put down

In conjugating verbs with accentuated prefixes
the latter are detached and put at the end of the
sentence: Ich mache die Thüre auf, Sie legen das Buch hin,
Er stellt den Stuhl hin, etc.

Bitte (bitte) please,   Danke (danke) I thank you

Remark 12: The accusative (= objective case) of
the masculines is formed by changing the ending of
articles,, pronouns and adjectives into n (respectively
adding en), the noun itself is not changed. The
feminine and neuter articles, pronouns and adjectives
do not undergo any change, ex. ·

Nominative: Der rothe Bleistift liegt hier
The red pencil lies here.

Accusative: Ich nehme den roten Bleistift
I take the red pencil.

Remark 13 : As said in remark 2, the pronoun "it" must be translated by er (he), ſie (she) when the noun is masculine or feminine; for the same reason the pronoun "it" must, in the accusative masc., be translated by ihn (him). Nehmen Sie den Bleiſtift? Ja, ich nehme ihn = Yes, I take it (him).

As there is no difference in the feminine between the nominative and accusative the English "she" and "her" are both in German "ſie."

an (an*) at, auf (ouf) on, unter (unt'r) under, vor (for) there, hinter (hin'tr) behind, neben (naib'n) near, in (in) in, zwiſchen (tsvish'n) between, hängen (haing'n) to hang, werfen (vairf'n) to throw, ziehen (tsee'n) to draw, ſtecken (shteck'n) to put into, to stick into, tragen (trahg'n) to carry.

Ich werfe (vairfə); er, ſie, es wirft (veerft); Sie werfen (vairf'n).

Ich trage (trahgə); er, ſie, es trägt (traigt); Sie tragen (trahg'n).

It will be noticed that for the third person singular the e in the stem of werfen is changed to i, and that the a of tragen is changed for the third person into ä; this change takes place in many verbs. We shall when they occur give the third person besides the infinitive or the first person.

Remark 14 : The objects of the above prepositions are in the accusative case (see remark 12).

Der Korb (korp) basket, der Überzieher (eebr'-tsee'r —'◡ —◡) overcoat, die Lehne (lainə) the back (of a chair), der Hacken (hahk'n) hook, die Zeitung (tsie-toong —' newspaper, die Ecke (eckə) corner.

---

* Sounds almost like the English on.

Remark 15 : The English "it" is often (especially after prepositions) translated by denſelben (accus. masc.), dieſelbe (fem.), daſſelbe (neut.), the literal meaning of which is "the same."

Sechſte Lektion (zextə) SIXTH LESSON.

1 (iens), 2 (tsvie), 3 (drie), 4 (feer), 5 (feenf), 6 (zex), 7 (zeeb'n), 8 (ahht), 9 (nien), 10 (tsain), 11 (elf), 12 (tsvœlf), 13 (drie'tsain), 14 (feer'tsain), 15 (feenf'tsain), 16 (zejh'tsain), 17 (zeeb'tsain), 18 (ahht'-tsain), 19 (nien'tsain), 20 (tsvan'tsijh), 21 (ien'-unt-tsvan'tsijh), 22 (tsvie'–unt–tsvan'tsijh), 23 (drie'–unt–tsvan'tsijh), 24 (feer'–unt–tsvan'tsijh), etc., 30 (drie'-sijh), 40 (feer'tsijh), 50 (feenf'tsijh), 60 (zejh'tsijh), 70 (zeeb'tsijh), 80 (ahht'tsijh), 90 nien'tsijh), 100 (hund'rt*), 200 (tsvie hund'rt), 365 (drie hund'rt feenf unt zejh'tsijh), 1000 (touz'nt). Zählen (tsail'n) to count. von (fon†) from, bis (biss) as far as, until, wie viel (vee-feel) how much, how many, mehr (mair) more, weniger (vai'nigr —'‿ ‿) less, noch weniger (nohh vai'nigr) still less, 3 mal 3 (drie mahl drie) 3 times 3, ebenſoviel (aib'n-zoh–feel) just as much, der Unterſchied (unt'r-sheet) difference.

The word um in sentences like "6 iſt um 2 mehr als 4" cannot be translated; it is used to show a difference in value but may be elided.

Masculine	Feminine	Neutre	
welcher	welche	welches	which
was für ein	was für eine	was für ein	what kind of a

* Don't forget to pronounce the u everywhere as in pull.
† Sounds almost like *fun*.

Notice the different forms of ein for the different genders ! Ein means *one* as well as *a* or *an*.

Remark 16 : When the English "what" is followed by a noun translate it by "what kind of," ex. : What hat is that ? Was für ein Hut ist das?

Remark 17 : After the indefinite article (ein, eine, ein) and the possessive pronouns (mein, Ihr, sein. etc.) the adjective takes the endings of the definite article (der, die, das) ex. : ein schwarzer Hut, eine schwarze Feder, ein schwarzes Kleid.

Die Einzahl (ien'tsahl(Singular
Die Mehrzahl (mair'tsahl) Plural.

Remark 18 : The plural of most nouns is formed by the ending e, a few however take er, and those ending in e (and a few monosyllables) take n or where euphony demands it en.

Masculines and neuters ending in *er*, *el*, *en* have the same form for the plural but often take the Umlaut, as : Fenster, Finger, Deckel, Haken, Kragen.

For examples in the formation of the plural see "Methode," page 19 and 20, for rules, see the appendix of this book.

Die Bürste brush, der Schüler (sheel'r) pupil (male), die Schülerin (sheel'rin) pupil (female), der Lehrer (lairər) teacher (male), die Lehrerin (lairərin) teacher (female), das Tuch (toohh) cloth, der Thermometer (tairmomait'r —⌣--'⌣) thermometer, der Federhalter penholder, der Deckel cover (of a book or a vessel), der Schlüssel (shleess'l) key, der Mantel (mant'l) cloak, der Nagel (nahg'l) nail.

Siebente Lektion (zeeb'ntə) SEVENTH LESSON.

PERSONAL PRONOUNS.

Nom. {	ich	er	sie	es	wir	Sie	sie
	I	he	she	it	we	you	they
Acc. {	mich	ihn	sie	es	uns	Sie	sie
	me	him	her	it	us	you	them

POSSESSIVE PRONOUNS.

mein	sein	ihr	sein	unser	Ihr	ihr
my	his	her	its	our	your	their

Remark 19 : As said in the 3rd lesson the possessive pronouns take an e when used as adjectives of feminine nouns, the same ending is used for the plural : meine Hände, Ihre Bleistifte, seine Bücher, etc.

The plural of der, die, das is die, as : das Buch the book, die Bücher, the books ; die Bleistifte the pencils, die Federn the pens.

The plural of dieser, jener, welcher for the three genders is diese, jene, welche.

The genitive plural of all these pronouns and articles ends in r, as : meiner Bücher of my books, der Damen of the ladies, dieser Schüler of the pupils (but dieses Schülers of this pupil [sing.]), welcher Herren of which gentlemen (but welches Herrn of which gentleman).

Remark 20 : The adjective preceded by an article or a pronoun ends in the plural in en, ex. : die schwarzen Bücher, meine großen Tische. But if the adjective is not preceded by an article or pronoun it ends in e for the nominative and accusative and in r for the genitive

(i. e. it has the ending which the article or pronoun would have had), ex. : ſchwarze Bücher, große Tiſche ;—blauer Augen of blue eyes, ſchwarzer Hüte of black hats.

Remark 21 : The verbs in the plural end in en.

ich gehe	wir gehen	er geht	ſie gehen
I go	we go	he goes	they go

ich habe	er hat	wir haben
(ijh hahbə)	(air hat)	(veer hahb'n)
I have	he has	we have

Sie haben	ſie haben
(zee hahb'n)	(zee hahb'n)
you have	they have

zuſammen	nur	mehrere	auch
(tsoozam'n —⌣'⌣)	(noor)	(mairərə —'⌣ ⌣)	(ouhh)
together	only	several	also

das Geld	die Mark	der Pfennig	ſehr
(gelt)	(mark)	(pfennijh)	(zair)
money	25 cents, 1 shilling	penny	very

viel	wenig	noch
(feel)	(vainijh)	(nohh)
much, many	little, few	still

kein	am meiſten	andere	beide
(kien)	(am miest'n)	(and rə)	(biedə)
not one, not any	the most	others	both

alle	einige	aber	die Schule
(allə)	(ienigə —'⌣⌣)	(ahb'r)	(shoolə)
all	some, a few	but	school

Aber and ſondern both mean *but;* the latter is only used to correct a previous statement.

18

Achte Lektion (ahhtə) EIGHTH LESSON.

schreiben	ich lese	er liest	sagen	heißen
(shrie'bn)	(laizə)	(leest)	(zahg'n)	(hie'ssn)
to write	I read	he reads	to say	to be called

enden	ich fange an	er fängt an	buchstabieren
(end'n)	(ijh fangə an)	(fangt*)	(boohh-stah-beer'n)
to end	I begin	he begins	to spell

sprechen	man spricht	antworten
(shprejh'n)	(man shprijht)	(ant'wortn)
to speak	one speaks	to answer

Remark 22: In English you often use *we, you* or *they* to speak indefinitely of people. as: "In Paris they speak French," in German man is used in such cases: Man spricht französisch in Paris.

ich stelle eine Frage	ich sage her
(ijh shtellə ienə frahgə)	(ijh zahgə hair)
I ask a question	I recite

der Buchstabe	die Silbe	das Wort	der Satz
(boohh-shtahbə —'— ⌣)	(zilbə)	(vorrt)	(zats)
letter	syllable	word	sentence

der Vokal	der Konsonant	die Seite
(vohkahl')	(kon-zoh-nant')	(zietə)
vowel	consonant	page

der Punkt	der Strich	das Fragezeichen
(punkt)	(shtrijh)	(frah-gə-tsie-jhən —'⌣—⌣)
period, point,	dash,	interrogation mark

---

* *ang* in fangt pronounced like *ang* in the English word *hang*.

das Ausrufzeichen	das Komma
(ous-roof-tsie-jhən —'———⌣)	(kom'mah)
exclamation mark	comma

auf deutsch	englisch	französisch
(ouf doitsh)	(ainglish)	(fran-tsœ-zish ⌣—'⌣)
in German	English	French

italienisch	spanisch	richtig	falsch
(ee-tahl–yai'-nish)	(shpah-nish)	(rijhtijh)	(falsh)
Italian	Spanish	correct	wrong

der erste, zweite, dritte, vierte, fünfte, the first, second, third, fourth, fifth (to form the ordinal numbers add te as far as nineteen incl., from twenty on add ste, as: zwanzigste, dreißigste, etc).

Remark 23: The ordinal numbers are declined like other adjectives, i. e. take the same endings for the cases or the plural.

Neunte Lektion (nointə) NINTH LESSON.

Die Übung (eebung) the exercise.

Der Schüler beantworte die folgenden Fragen.
(dair shee-l'r bai-ant'-vor-tə dee fol'gen-dn frah-gn
The student is to answer the following questions.

Der Schüler bilde die zu den folgenden Antworten passenden Fragen.
(dair sheel'r bildə dee tsoo dain fol'-gen-dn ant'-vor-tn
    pass'n-dn frah-g'n)
The student is to form the questions fitting the following answers.

Zehnte Lektion (tsaintə) TENTH LESSON.

stellen	stehen	setzen	sitzen	schieben
to put	to stand	to set	to sit	to push

bleiben	lassen	er läßt
(blieb'n)	(lass'n)	(laisst)
to remain	to leave	he leaves

Wohin (voh-hin — ‿')?   Wo (voh)?
Whither (where to)?   Where (at what place)?

Woher (voh-hair — —')?
Whence (where from)?

Remark 24: In German you must carefully distinguish between whither, where and whence. You cannot say: Where are you going? instead of: Whither are you going? (= where are you going to?)

Remark 25: After the verb "to be" the nominative is used; after prepositions denoting a motion towards a place (i e. answering the question "whither?, where to?) the accusative is used; after prepositions denoting the occupying of a place (where is it?) and those signifying leaving or going away (whence?) the dative follows. As the same preposition sometimes may denote a motion towards a place (I put the book on [under] the table), or the occupation of a place (the book lies on [under] the table) the accusative or the dative must follow according to the meaning. See examples in the "Methode" page 29 of the nominative after the question "Was ist das?", the accusative after "Wohin?", the dative after "Woher?" and "Wo?"

Remark 26 : The dative singular of articles and pronominal adjectives is formed in the masculine by the ending m (dem, welchem, diesem, etc.), in the feminine by the ending r (der, welcher, einer, meiner, etc.); the adjectives preceded by articles or pronominal adjectives end in n (dem großen Bleistift, der schwarzen Feder, dem grünen Buch), but ·if not thus preceded they take the ending of the article (schwarzem Haar, roter Tinte, grünem Buch). The masculine and neuter nouns, if they have not already an e in the last syllable, may take an e* (dem Stuhle, dem Tische, dem Buche, but dem Boden without e as there is one in the last syllable); feminine nouns remain unchanged. The dative plural of all words for all genders ends in n (den langen Bleistiften, diesen großen Thüren, jenen breiten Fenstern).

die Karte (dee karrtə) card	das Schulzimmer (das shool'-tsim-mr) schoolroom	das Vorzimmer fohr'-tsim-mr) anteroom
die Schublade (shoob'-lah-də) drawer	heraus (hair-ous ⌣⌣') out (adv.)	hinein (hin-ien ⌣⌣') in (adv.)
der Brief (dair breef) letter	der Schirm (sheerm) umbrella, parasol	der Regenschirm (raig'n-sheerm) umbrella
das Sofa (zohfah) sofa	etwas (et'-vass) something	nichts (nijhts) nothing	jemand (yai'-mant) somebody

niemand ·
(nee'-mant)
nobody

heraus
(hairous ⌣—')
out of it

---

* This e may also be omitted.

Personal Pronouns.

	Whom?	me	him	her	it	us	you	them
Acc.	Wen?	mich	ihn	fie	es	uns	Sie	fie
Dat.	Wem?	mir	ihm	ihr	ihm	uns	Ihnen	ihnen

Remark 27. "Myself" and "ourselves" are translated like "me" and "us." (Ich lege das Buch vor mich [uns] I lay the book in front of myself [ourselves]).

Yourself, himself, herself, itself, yourselves, themselves are all translated by fich, ex. : er legt es neben fich = he puts it near himself; ftellen Sie das Tintefaß vor fich = put the inkstand in front of yourself; die Herren halten das Buch zwischen fich = the gentlemen hold the book between themselves.

"To sit down" is translated by fich feßen (literally : to set one's self) : Ich feße mich, er (fie) feßt fich, wir feßen uns, Sie feßen fich, fie feßen fich.

Elfte Lektion (elftə) Eleventh Lesson.

können (kœnnən)	to be able	müffen (meess'n)	to be obliged
ich kann (kan)	I can	ich muß (muss)	I must
er kann	he can	er muß	he must
wir können	we can	wir müffen	we must
fie können*	they can	fie müffen	they must

wollen (voll'n)	to desire	ich drehe an (ab)
ich will (vill)	I desire	(draihə an (ap)
er will	he desires	I turn on (off)
wir wollen	we desire	ich hebe auf
fie wolleu	they desire	(haibə ouf)
		I lift (up)

---

*As the translation of "you" is the same as for "they" (only that the former is spelt with a capital) we shall not any more give both in the conjugations.

Remark 28 : Infinitives stand at the end of the sentence in which case adverbs forming only one idea with the verb are written together with it. like prefixes, as : Ich drehe das Gas an (I turn the gas on) but : Ich will das Gas andrehen (I desire to turn on the gas), in the latter example drehen being an infinitive (since it depends on another verb = will) Such prefixes are called separable and are always accented.

zu	genug	schwer	leicht
(tsoo)	(gənoohh ‿—’)	(shvair)	(liejht)
too	enough	heavy	light

stark	schwach	dazu
(shtarrk)	(shvahh)	(dah-tsoo’)
strong	weak˙	for it

ich schließe zu	ich schließe auf	verschlossen
(shleessə tsoo)	(shleessə ouf)	(fərshloss’n)
I lock	I unlock	locked

zerreißen	verschneiden
(tsər-rie’-ssn)	(tsər-shnie’-dn)
to tear	to cut

zerbrechen	steigen
(tsər-brejh’n)	(shtie’gn)
to break	to step up (or down)

Remark 29 : ''For'' referring to verbs is translated by um zu (for writing = um zu schreiben. Are you tall enough for reaching the gas fixture = Sind Sie groß genug, um den Gasarm zu berühren).

''For'' with nouns and pronouns is für (followed by the accusative as : für mich, für Sie, für ihn, für den Herrn, für die Frau).

der obere Rahmen	die Konsole	die Uhr
(oh-bə-rə rahm'n)	(kon-zoh'-lə)	(oor)
the upper frame	shelf	the watch, clock

die Pappe	die Bank	das Nebenzimmer
(pap-pə)	(bank*)	(naib'n-tsim-mr)
the paste-board	the bench	adjoining room

das Wörterbuch	die Handtasche	der Platz
(vœr-tər-boohh —'- —)	(hant'-tashe*)	(platts)
the dictionary	the hand-bag	the place

jawohl	links von Ihnen	warum
(yah-vohl')	(links fon ee-nən)	(vah-rum'†)
yes, indeed	on your left	why

weil	wenn	ohne
(viel)	(ven)	(ohnə)
because	if	without

Remark 30 : After most conjunctions ‡ the verb is transposed to the end of the sentence, the adverbs spoken of in remark 28 being used as prefixes in such cases. Compare the following :

without conjunction { ich mache die Thür auf
                     { die Decke ist weiß

with conjunction { wenn ich die Thür aufmache
                  { wenn die Decke weiß ist
                  { weil ich die Thür aufmache
                  { weil die Decke weiß ist

---

*Pronounce the *a* as in *yacht*.   † u as in *pull*.
‡ i. e. all those introducing subordinate clauses,

Remark 31: Many adverbs are formed with hin and her, as: hinein, herein (into) hinauf, herauf (up); hinunter, herunter (down); hinab, herab (down); hinaus, heraus (out)—her conveying the idea of direction towards the speaker. hin the direction away from the speaker, as: Kommen Sie herein = come in (I am in the room myself), but: Gehen Sie hinein = go in (I am outside).

Zwölfte Lektion (tsvœlftə) TWELFTH LESSON.

Geben (gaib'n) to give; er giebt (gipt) he gives; erhalten (erhalt'n) to receive; er erhält (erhell't) he receives; reichen (riejh'n) to reach, to pass; bringen to bring; bitten um to ask for, to beg for; schicken to send; danken to thank; sagen to say; weit davon entfernt (wiet da-fon' ent-fairnt') far away from it; der Name (nahmə) the name; das Bild (bilt) the picture; das Streichholz (shtriejh'holts) the match (plural: die Streichhölzer); durch (doorjh) through.

Another is translated by ein anderer (nomin. masc.), einen anderen (accus. masc.), eine andere (fem.) ein anderes (neut.).

Remark 32: When a verb has two objects, an indirect and a direct one (i. e. a personal and an impersonal one), the former takes the dative form (see remark 26, as also the declension table in the appendix). Examples: Ich gebe dem Herrn den Bleistift. Er reicht der Frau die Feder, Geben Sie mir (not: mich) meinen Hut, Ich sage Ihnen (not: Sie) meinen Namen.

Remark 33: Myself, yourself, etc., as reflexive pronouns, i. e. when subject and object represent the same person (as in: he puts it before himself, he seats himself; er stellt es vor sich, er setzt sich) have been explained in remark 27, but when they merely serve to emphasize who the person is, the word ſelbſt is used. Ex. : Ich komme ſelbſt, I am coming myself ; er ſchreibt das ſelbſt, he himself is writing it ; er ſchickt es ihr ſelbſt, he is sending it to her herself. &c.

Etwas some, a little ; bitte means *please* or *you are welcome* (after receiving thanks) ; Seien Sie ſo gütig (zie'n zee zoh geetijh) be so kind ; Haben Sie die Güte (geetə) have the kindness.

Remark 34 : Translate : *tell him to do it* by *tell him that he shall do it*=Sagen Sie ihm, daß er es thun ſoll. The conjunction may be elided : Tell him he shall do it=Sagen Sie ihm, er ſoll es thun.

Remark 35 : After the conjunction daß the verb is put at the end of the clause (compare remark 30).

Ich ſoll, er ſoll, wir ſollen, ſie ſollen ; though ſollen has often the meaning of *shall* it frequently has other meanings especially *to be desired to do a thing.* Examples : Ich ſoll ſchreiben, They desire me to write ; Sie ſollen gehen, you are desired to go ; Karl ſoll die Thür zumachen, I want Charles to close the door.

Dreizehnte Lektion (drie-tsaintə) THIRTEENTH LESSON.

Remark 36 : The prepositions mit (*with*), zu (*to*) are always followed by the dative. The word was is rarely used after prepositions, wo (before vowels wor) contracted with the preposition is used instead : womit with what, wovon from what, wofür for what, worin in what, worauf on what, etc.

ſchneiden	er ſchneidet	ſehen	er ſieht	hören
(shnie'dn)	(shniedət)	(zai'n)	(zeet)	(hœr'n)
to cut	he cuts	to see	he sees	to hear

riechen   essen   er ißt   trinken   klopfen
(reejh'n)   (ess'n)   (isst)   (trink'n)   (klopf'n)
to smell   to eat   he eats   to drink   to knock

laut   leise   schnell   langsam   gut   besser
(lout)   (liesə)   (shnell)   (lang'zahm)   (goot)   (bess'r)
loud   low   quick   slow   good   better

am besten   schlecht   die Blume   die Rose   die Tulpe
(am best'n)   (shlejht)   (bloomə)   (rohzə)   (tulpə)
the best   bad   flower   rose   tulip

das Veilchen   das Stiefmütterchen   die Vase
(fieljh'n)   (shteef-meet'rjh'n—'—⌣⌣)   (vahzə)
violet   pansy   vase

der Apfel   die Birne   die Traube   das Brot   das Fleisch
((apf'l)   (beernə)   (traubə)   (broht)   (fliesh)
apple   pear   grape   bread   meat

die Erdbeere   die Kirsche   die Frucht (pl. Früchte)   das Obst
(airt'bairə)   (keershə)   (fruhht) (freejhtə)   (ohpst)
strawberry   cherry   fruit   fruit

das Gemüse   die Speise   das Getränk   der Kaffee
(gemeezə)   (shpiezə)   (getrenk')   (kaffai)
vegetable   food   drink   coffee

der Thee   die Milch   das Wasser   der Wein   das Bier
(tai)   (miljh)   (vass'r)   (vien)   (beer)
tea   milk   water   wine   beer

die Limonade   die Bohne   die Erbse   die Kartoffel   die Butter
(limonah'də)   (bohnə)   (erpsə)   (kartoff'l)   (boott'r)
limonade   bean   pea   potato   butter

der Zucker   her-sagen   man nennt
(tsoock'r)   (hair zahg'n—'—⌣)   (mann nennt)
sugar   to recite, ich sage her I recite   one names (calls)

Vierzehnte Lektion (feer-tsaintə) FOURTEENTH LESSON.

Vor dem Essen	das Tischtuch	jeder	die Person
before eating	(tish'-toohh)	(yaid'r)	(pairzoh'n)
	table cloth	every	person

der Teller	rund	viereckig	die Schüssel	der Löffel
(tell'r)	(runt)	(feer'-eckijh)	(sheess'l)	(lœffl)
plate	round	square	dish	spoon

die Gabel	das Messer	das Glas	die Flasche	die Tasse	gießen
(gahb'l)	(mess'r)	(glahs)	(nash'ə)	(tass'ə)	(gees'n)
fork	knife	glass	bottle	cup	to pour

Remark 37: The word "of" in expressions like a glass of water. a piece of paper, is not translated (ein Glas Wasser, ein Stück Papier).

schmecken	der Geschmack	der Geruch	die Zunge
(shmeck'n)	(gəshm'ıck')	(gəroohh')	(tsoongə)
to taste	taste	smell	tongue

bitter	sauer	süß
(bittr)	(zou'r)	(zees)
bitter	sour	sweet)

angenehm	unangenehm
(an'·gənaim)	('— — ◡ —)
agreeable. pleasant	disagreeable, unpleasant

gern mögen (gairn mœg'n) to like — ich mag (mahh) I like
nicht mögen not to like — er mag he likes
gern essen to like to eat — wir mögen we like
" trinken " drink — sie mögen they like
" riechen " smell
lieber mögen (leeb'r) to like better, to prefer
lieber trinken to prefer drinking
am liebsten mögen (am leebst'n) to like best

schön	häßlich	schmutzig	zerrissen
(shœn)	(hess'lijh)	(shmoot'sijh)	(tserriss'n)
beautiful	ugly	dirty	torn

der Einband	eingebunden	der Teppich
(ien'bant)	(iengəbundn —'⌣ ⌣ ⌣)	(teppijh)
binding	bound	carpet

das Stück	holen	die Speisekarte
(shteeck)	(hohl'n)	(spiezə-karrtə —⌣ ⌣'⌣)
piece	to fetch	bill of fare

die Portion	die Zuckerdose
(ports-yoh'n)	(tsoockr-dohsə)
portion	sugar bowl

Die Uhr (oor) THE TIMEPIECE (Watch or Clock)

Konsole (konzohlə ⌣—'⌣) bracket, verschieden (fer shee'dn) different, Wanduhr (vant-oor) hanging clock. Standuhr (shtant-oor) standing clock, Stutzuhr (shtuts-oor) French clock, Taschenuhr (tash'n-oor) watch, der Zeiger (tsie'gr) the hand of a clock or watch, zeigen (tsie'gn) to show, to point out, die Stunde (shtundə) the hour, die Minute (minnoo'tə) the minute, die Sekunde (zeckun'də) the second, der Tag (tahh) the day.

Ich ziehe meine Uhr auf I wind up my watch, ich stelle meine Uhr I set my watch, nach behind time, vor ahead of time. die Uhr geht vor the watch gains, sie geht nach it looses, sie geht richtig it is on time. gerade (gərah'də) exactly.

Wieviel Uhr ist es? What time is it? Um wieviel Uhr? At what time? Ein Uhr, zwei Uhr, drei Uhr one o'clock, two o'clock, three o'clock. Ein Viertel (feertl) one quarter, halb (halp) half, dreiviertel three quarters.*

Besides saying as in English a quarter past (nach), a quarter before (vor), 5 minutes to (bis), it is common in German instead ¼ or ½ past an hour, or ¼ before an hour to say ¼, ½, ¾ toward the next hour, for instance ¼ past two would be ¼ toward 3 = ein Viertel auf drei ; half past two = halb drei ; ¼ to three = dreiviertel auf drei.

Anfangen to commence. zu Ende sein to terminate, dauern (dour'n) to last, enthalten to contain, Kaminsims (kameen'-zims) mantle shelf, im Gegenteil (—'‿—) on the contrary, woraus out of what (i. e. what is it made of).

Stoffnamen names of substances, das Metall' the metal, Gold gold, Silber silver, Kupfer copper, Messing brass, Eisen iron, Blei lead, Seide silk, Sammet velvet, Wolle (volle) wool, Baumwolle (boum-volle) cotton, Leinwand (lien-vant) linnen, Leder leather, Holz wood, Stein stone, Marmor marble.

When names of substances are used as adjectives they have the ending en or ern, as : golden golden, bleiern leaden, seiden silken, etc . besides this ending they have the declension endings like other adjectives, as : der hölzerne Tisch, ein hölzerner Tisch.

Das Jahr. THE YEAR.

Bilden to form, der Tag the day, einteilen (ich teile in.. ein) to divide into, der Monat (moh'nat) the month, die Woche the week. sie heißen they are called, der Sonntag Sunday, der Montag Monday, der Dienstag (deens'tahh) Tuesday. der Mittwoch Wednesday, der Donnerstag Thursday. der Freitag

---

*Das drittel, fünftel, sechstel, u. s. w. the third, fifth, sixth, etc. to form fractional numbers add l to the ordinals.

Friday, der Sonnabend (zon'ahbnd) (Samstag) Saturday,
arbeiten (ar'bietn) to work, der Ruhetag (roo'e-tahh) day of
rest, einige some, dieser Monate of these months (genit.
plur.), allein (alie'n) only, also therefore, solcher=e=es (zoljh'r)
such, das Schaltjahr leap year, die Jahreszeit season, der
Frühling (free'ling) spring, der Sommer summer, der Herbst
autumn (fall), der Winter winter, enthalten (ent-halt'n) to
contain, heute (hoitə) to-day, gestern (gest'rn) yesterday,
war was, morgen (morg'n) to-morrow,

Page 59 ; der wievielste (vee-feel-stə) which (referring
to ordinal numbers only), nachschlagen (ich schlage nach) to
look up, der Kalender (‿‿'‿) calendar, almanac, Sehen
Sie her (hair) look here, vorig last, previous, nächst
(pronounce as in English) next, fallen to fall, fällt falls,
darum (‿‿') therefore, die Aufgabe (ouf'gah-bə) exercise,
schlagen to strike.

Übung : Der wievielste ist (den wievielsten haben wir) what
day of the month is it? welche auf den Winter folgt, which
follows winter ; jetzt, now.
Ich komme 3 mal die Woche hierher. I come here 3 times a
week ; es giebt, there are ; die dem Herbst vorangeht (for-an'-
gait) which precedes autumn.

Remark 38 : As relative pronouns, the various
forms of der, die, das or welcher, welche, welches are used both
for persons or things : der Mann, der (or welcher) in das
Zimmer kommt, the man who comes into the room ;
der Wein, der (or welcher) auf dem Tische steht, the wine which
is on the table ; der Bleistift, den (or welchen) ich nehme, the
pencil which I take ; der Mann, den (welchen) ich sehe ; die
Frau, die (welche) mir ein Buch giebt—der Mann, von dem (welchem)
ich spreche of whom I am speaking.

Remember: 1) that in a relative clause the verb must stand at the end; 2) that the relative pronoun cannot be omitted, example: the money (which) I have in my pocket, das Geld, welches (or das) ich in meiner Tasche habe.

In the genitive sing. and plur. and dative plural the forms of the article or of welch... are not used; the following must be employed: *Genit. sing. masc.* or *neut.*: der Mann, dessen Freund ich bin, the man whose friend I am; das Kleid, dessen Farbe grün ist, the dress, the color of which is green; *genit. fem.* and *genit. plur.* for all genders: die Frau, deren Hut ich habe the lady whose hat I have; die Herren, deren Freunde wir sind, the gentlemen whose friends we are; *dative plur. for all genders:* die Herren, denen wir das Geld geben. the gentlemen to whom we give the money.

Tag und Nacht. DAY AND NIGHT.

Teilen to divide, der Teil part, während (vair'nt *followed by the genitive*) during, hell light, dunkel dark, an'zünden to light, das Streichholz the match, brennen to burn, jetzt now. beleuchten or erleuchten (erloijht'n) to light up. illuminate. zu nahe kommen to get too near, die Flamme the flame, verbrennen to scorch, burn, daher (dah-hair) therefore.

Page 61: der Saal (*plural* Säle) the hall, die Sonne the sun, die am Himmel ist which is in the sky, schauen (shou'n) to look, sichtbar visible, der Mond the moon, der Stern (shtairn) the star, der Anfang des Tages the beginning of day, der Morgen the morning, desselben of it, of the same. der Abend the evening, geht auf rises, geht unter sets, der Mittag noon, dem Süden gegenüber liegt lies opposite the south, der Often the east, der Weften the west, der Norden the north, der Süden the south, die Himmelsgegend cardinal point, früh early, fpät late, auf'ftehen (ich ftehe auf) to rise, get up, an'kleiden (ich kleide mich an) to dress, frühftücken to breakfast.

Übung: Um fehen zu können in order to be able to see, das der Sonne that of the sun, die Sonne scheint the sun shines.

Das Wetter. THE WEATHER.

Die Wolke cloud, bedeckt covered, regnen to rain, der Tropfen the drop, der Regenschirm the umbrella, gegen against, oben above, es geht fich fchlecht walking is bad, gefchützt (gesheetst') protected, die Straße (shtrah'sə) the street, der Schritt the step, befpritzen bespatter, zurück'kehren to return, um aus'zugehen for going out, wechfeln to change, naß wet, aus'ziehen to take off, trocken dry, an'ziehen put on, fchneien to snow, die Schneeflocke the snowflake, gemifcht mixed, fchlagen to beat, die Fensterscheibe the window pane.

Page 64: Ich wärme mich I get warm (warm myself), die Kohle the coal, halten to hold, es friert mich (Sie, ihn, uns, etc.) I (you, etc) feel cold, es ift mir (Ihnen, ihm, ihr, etc.) warm I (you, etc.) feel warm, winbig windy, feft'halten to hold fast, um'klappen to turn inside out, noch still. vertreiben to disperse, auch also, oft often, felten seldom, nie never, immer always, zuweilen sometimes, fcheinen to shine.

Remark 39: Prepositions are frequently con-tracted with the article; as vom=von bem, am=an dem, im = in dem, zur = zu ber; beim= bei dem.

Übung. Bei fchlechtem Wetter in bad weather, vom Himmel from the sky, der Schmuz the dirt, fchützen vor (with dative) to protect against, draußen out of doors, heizen to heat, die Kälte the cold, die Wärme the warmth, (in the same way nouns are formed from other adjectives, i. e. die Länge, die Größe, die Schwere, etc.), vorbei' gehen to go past, der Schatten the shade.

Die Vergangenheit (fərgang'n-hiet) THE PAST.

Remark 40 : The past is formed as in English by the auxiliary *have* and the past participle, but not only the English "perfect" is translated by the German "perfect" but often also the English "imperfect," thus : Ich habe es gethan means not only *I have done it* or *I have been doing it* but also *I did it* or *I was doing it*.

The past participles of simple verbs (except those ending in iren) have the prefix ge (as : Infinitive tragen, past participle getragen), those having already an unaccented prefix do not take the ge (as : Infinitive erhalten ‿‿'‿, past participle unchanged), those having an accented prefix take the ge between prefix and root (as : anfangen‿'‿ ‿, angefangen ‿'‿ ‿'‿).

The participles of some verbs end in t (called the weak, new, or t–conjugation), of others in n (called the strong, old, or n–conjugation). These conjugations correspond in a great measure with the English regular or irregular conjugations, thus : *danced, learned, lived* are getanzt, gelernt, gelebt, but *seen, spoken, written* are gesehen, gesprochen, geschrieben. In n-participles the radical vowel is often changed (as in English : *sing, sung, break, broken*), *in* becoming *un*, as : trinken, getrunken, binden (bin'dn, to tie) gebunden; ei (pronounce like ie in "die") in a short syllable becoming i (pronounce as i in "sister"), in a long one ie (pronounce as ee in "meet") ſchneiden, geſchnitten, ſchreiben, geſchrieben ; e if followed by two consonants (except ſſ) becomes o, if followed by one consonant or ſſ it remains : brechen gebrochen, werfen geworfen, leſen geleſen, meſſen (to measure) gemeſſen, helfen (to help) geholfen ; sometimes i becomes e and ie becomes o : ſitzen geſeſſen, bitten gebeten, ſchieben geſchoben, frieren gefroren, ſchließen geſchloſſen, riechen gerochen.

Remember that the participles of ſtehen, liegen, ziehen, nehmen, eſſen, bringen are : geſtanden, gelegen, gezogen, genommen, gegeſſen, gebracht (see the list of participles in the foot note of page 67 of the method).

Remark 41 : Wollen, können, müſſen which literally mean *will, can, must* have in English no past participle nor infinitive (you cannot say : I have *would*, I have *could*, I hope to *can*, etc., you substitute in such case a synonymous expression, as : I have desired, I have been able, I hope to be able, etc.) but they have these forms in German : Ich habe gekonnt "I have been able" or "I could" Er hat gewollt "he has desired " or "he wanted." Wir haben gemußt "we were obliged to."

Remark 42 : When the participles of these verbs (können, wollen, müſſen) and a few others, especially the verb laſſen (to let or to leave), are accompanied by an infinitive, the infinitive of these verbs is used instead of the participle in forming the past, thus :

No infinitive:	*Accompanied by an infinitive:*
Ich habe das Buch gewollt.	Ich habe leſen wollen.
I wanted the book.	I wanted to read.
Haben Sie das gekonnt ?	Nein, ich habe nicht ſehen können.
Were you capable (of) it ?	No, I was not able to see.

Pages 66, 67, 68: frei free ; treten Sie ein step in,
enter; das Packet' the package ; bei uns gelaſſen haben have
left at our house ; draußen out of doors ; ab'gelegt taken
off ; auch besides ; ſchon already ; eben just ; gar nicht not at
all ; die Zeit the time ; noch nicht ganz not quite ; durch'leſen
to read over ; mit nach Hauſe genommen taken home with
(him)—the object after mit is often elided—; ſein kleiner
Junge his little boy (son) ; die Abweſenheit the absence ;
ab'halten to keep from ; alſo, guten Morgen well then, good
morning ; Abieu good bye.

Remark 43 : Bei mir, bei Ihnen, bei ihm, bei dem Herrn, bei
der Frau mean : at my house, at your house, at his
house, etc.

Vergangenheit.

Fortſetzung (fort'-zets-oong) continuation

Remark 44 : The past of "to be" (been geweſen
gəvaiz'n) is not formed with the auxiliary "to have"
but "to be," I have been, we (you, they) have been,
he has been, is therefore : Ich bin geweſen, wir (Sie, ſie) ſind
geweſen, er iſt geweſen (literally : I am been, you are been,
he is been, etc.

In the same manner is formed the past of bleiben=
to remain and of such intransitive verbs as denote a
change of place, as : gehen, kommen, fahren to ride in a
vehicle, reiten to ride on horseback, reiſen to travel,
abreiſen to start on a journey, ankommen to arrive, ſteigen
to step up *or* down, eintreten to step into, to enter,
aus'treten to step out, fallen to fall, aufſtehen to rise, etc.
The past participles are : gegangen, gekommen, gefahren,
geritten, gereiſt, abgereiſt, angekommen, geſtiegen, eingetreten, ausge=
treten, gefallen, aufgeſtanden. The prefixes an, ab, auf, aus ein

have the heavy accent, thus the infinitives are —'— ⌣, the participles —'⌣—⌣.

Remark 45 : Verbs denoting a change of condition (in English often expressed with *get*) form their past also with *to be*, as : zerbrechen to get broken, zerreißen to get torn, erkalten to get cold, werden to become. Der Stuhl ist zerbrochen the chair has gotten broken, die Suppe ist erkaltet the soup has gotten cold, das Wetter ist schön geworden the weather has become fine.

Page 69 : sich verabschieden (fer-ap'-sheedn) to take leave; sogleich (zoh-gliejh') immediately, at once; der Bahnhof the station, depot; sie sind die Treppe herauf'gekommen they have come upstairs; Hat er sich einen Arm gebrochen? has he broken his arm ?; hat erst zu weinen angefangen only began to cry.

Remark 46 : For parts of the body the reflexive mir, sich is generally used instead of the possessive my, your, etc., as : ich habe mich in den Finger geschnitten I have cut my finger.

Page 70 : nun ja very well; dann then; schlimm bad; gestern Abend last night; im Theater in the theatre; erst gegen acht only towards eight; Kurz nach dem Essen shortly after dinner ; ich muß jetzt fort I must (go) away now ; Ich will zu Karl I will (go) to Charles.

Remark 47 : After müssen, wollen, the verbs *go*, *come*, are elided, after können also the verb *speak* Wollen Sie in das Theater? do you want to go to the theatre? Ich kann Deutsch I can speak German.

Übung : Esse ein Brötchen (broet'-jh'n) dazu eat a roll with it; auf meine Stube (shtoobə) to my room; der Fehler the mistake ; er geht fort he goes away ; den Nach'mittag über through the afternoon ; im Freien out of doors ; sie treten aber nicht ein but they do not enter; das Bibliothekzimmer (beeb-lee-oh-taik'-tsimr) the library; Begleitet man does one accompany?

Die Zukunft (tsookoonft—'⌣) THE FUTURE

Remark 48 : The future in German is not formed by *shall, will* or *to be going to*, but by werden=to become. Example : Ich werde morgen kommen (ijh vairdə) I shall come to-morrow. Werden Sie ins Theater gehen (vaird'n zee) will you go to the theatre? Er wird das Buch nehmen (air veert) he will take the book. Wir werden um ein Uhr essen (veer vaird'n) we shall eat at one o'clock. Sie werden nächste Woche den Brief erhalten you will receive the letter next week. Werden die Kinder in die Schule gehen? will the children go to school?

Remark 49 : Notice that the infinitive stands at the end of the sentence.

Remark 50 : The future of können, wollen, müssen is formed in the regular way, though lacking in English: Ich werde können I shall be able, Sie werden ins Theater gehen müssen you will be obliged to go to the theatre, er wird bleiben wollen he will desire to remain.

Remark 51 : When the English *shall* denotes obligation and *will* denotes desire, they are rendered in German by sollen and wollen : You shall do it Sie sollen es thun, I will (intend to) do it ich will es thun.

Page 71: übrig bleibt remains to spare; mit'kommen come along; die Kinder (sing. das Kind) the children ; täglich daily ; wir wollen sie nicht ab'halten we will not keep them from it; Gehen sie gern? Do they like to go? (Do they go willingly ?) Ende nächster Woche at the end of next week ; folgenden following, next; vor der Abreise before your departure ; ich werde bleiben können I shall be able to remain.

Die Tiere. ANIMALS.

Das Tier the animal, das Wesen the being, belebt animate, unbelebt inanimate, zu denen to whom, gehören belong to, um zu leben in order to live (for living), atmen to breathe, die Luft the air, die Nahrung the nourishment, sterben to die, lebend living, der Sinn the sense, das Gesicht the sight, das Gehör the hearing, der Geruch the smell, der Geschmack the taste, das Gefühl the feeling, das Werkzeug (instrument) organ, diejenigen des Gehörs those of hearing, der Sitz the seat.

Page 73 : der Gaumen palate, verbreiten spread, wahrnehmen to notice, to perceive (with any of the 5 senses), die Gestalt the shape, die Ausdehnung extension (dimension), die Lage position, der Gegenstände (genit. plur.) of the objects, der Ort the place.

Remark 52 : Sich befinden to be (used only of place, or health, as : Er befindet sich hier he is here ; ich befinde mich wohl I am well ; wir befinden uns nicht wohl we are not well ; wie befinden Sie sich how are you ?)

Vernehmen to perceive (with the ears), der Laut the sound, empfinden to feel, das Eis the ice, der Schmerz the pain, bemerken to observe, to notice, weich soft, hart hard, die Art the kind, hauptsächlich principal, die Vierfüßler the quadrupeds, der Vogel the bird, der Fisch the fish, das Reptil the reptile, das Amphibium amphibious animal, das Insekt insect, festes Land terra firma (mainland), laufen to run, springen to jump, folgend following, das Pferd the horse, der Ochs the ox, die Kuh the cow, der Esel the donkey, das Schaf the sheep, der Hund the dog, die Katze the cat, das Haustier domestic animal, der Löwe the lion, der Tiger the tiger, der Bär the bear, die Hyäne the hyena, der Wolf the wolf, der Fuchs the fox, wild wild, außer (with Dative) besides, der

Flügel the wing, fliegen to fly, ſtatt (with Genitive) instead, der Schnabel the bill (beak), die Feder the feather, das Huhn the chicken, die Ente the duck, die Gans the goose, der Pfau the peacock, der Adler the eagle, der Strauß the ostrich, die Eule the owl, die Schwalbe the swallow, der Sperling the sparrow, oben above, beſchrieben described, das Blut the blood, das Herz the heart, zirkulieren to circulate, die Lunge the lung, der Magen the stomach, verdauen to digest, krank sick.

Page 74: die Floſſe the fin, ſchwimmen to swim, die Schuppe the scale, bekannt known, die Schlange the snake, kriechen to creep, der Erdboden the ground (earth), der Froſch the frog, die Biene the bee, der Honig the honey, die Seidenraupe the silk worm, nützlich useful, die Fliege the fly, Mücke the mosquito, ſchädlich destructive.

Übung: Was geſchieht what happens, gedeihen prosper. 6. kannteſten most known, ſieht aus looks like, zahm tame. Geſundheit health, geſund healthy, ſich fort'bewegen move about.

Gehören *to belong* is followed by the dative without preposition to denote *possession*, as: das Haus gehört dem Mann, das Pferd gehört mir, but the preposition zu is used when *belong* denotes *classification*, as: das Pferd gehört zu den Haustieren.

Der Menſch (MAN, HUMAN BEING.)

Scharf acute (sharp), das Gehirn brain, entwickeln to develop, denken an (accus.) to think of (past, gedacht), bilden form, der Geiſt the mind (spirit), der Gedanke thought, ausdrüken to express, abweſend absent, jemand somebody, Verſtand intelligence, beanlagt talented, die Anlage talent, lernen (lairnən) to learn, grammatikaliſch grammatical, wiſſen to know, (Ich weiß [vies], er weiß, wir wissen) sie stehen eingetragen they have been entered, behalten to retain, es giebt Dinge there are things, entgehen escape wieder (veedr) again, vergessen forget, das Geschlecht the gender, einige some (einiger of some), Beim Menschen with mankind, das Gefühl feeling, die Empfindung sensation, die Bewunderung admiration, das Schöne beauty, der Widerwille repugnance, das Häßliche ugliness, einen Wunsch hegen to have a desire, besitzen to possess, gerne mögen to like, hoffen to hope, in Erfüllung gehen to be fulfilled, wünschen to wish, nächst next, geläufig fluently, bei dem Gedanken at the thought, geschehen happen, die Furcht the fear, fürchten to fear, die Aufgabe exercise, task, tadeln censure, scold, erfahren experience. die Freude joy, das Bedauern regret, der Fortschritt progress, der Fehler fault, mistake, sich freuen über to rejoice at, versäumen to miss, es thut mir leid I am sorry.

Übung page 77 : überlegen sein to be superior, gedacht thought, ob if, whether, gewußt known, betrachten to look at, contemplate, reich rich, ich erkälte mich I catch cold, (Sie erkälten sich).

Die Einladung (ien'lah-doong) INVITATION.

Ich lade ein I invite, das Vergnügen pleasure, besuchen to visit, da as, die Hauptstadt capital (city), das Land country, verlassen to leave, schön all right, abreisen set out, depart, wenn es Ihnen recht ist if it suits you, Ich bin es zufrieden I am satisfied (willing).

Remark 53 : to is translated by nach in speaking of countries or cities.

Reisen to go (travel), das Dampfschiff steamer, die Elbe hinauf up the Elbe, sächsische Schweiz Saxon Switzerland,

Oesterreich Austria, fahren to go, to proceed, bis as far as, die Eisenbahn railway, die Fahrt trip (ride), dauern to last, halb half, die Reise journey, voyage, der Berg mountain, die Alpen the Alps, ab'brechen break off, shorten, der Fahrplan time-table, nach'sehen look up, der Zug train, verzeichnet marked, scheduled, der Eilzug express train, günstig favorable, noch still, an'sehen to visit, inspect, ab'holen to call for, packen pack, heute noch to-day yet, fertig ready, besorgen to arrange, to settle, auf morgen until to-morrow, auf Wieder= sehen au revoir.

Übung, page 79: sich treffen to meet, nachdem after, ladet ein invites, noch niemals never yet; sie trennen sich they separate.

Remark 54: The conjunction indem and the verb are translated with *by* and the present participle, as: indem ich esse by eating, indem sie nach Berlin fahren by travelling to Berlin, nachsehen to look up.

Überschrieben entitled, wohnen to reside, Durchreise passing through, das Volk (pl. die Völker) the people, nation, bewohnen inhabit, Sprache language, sie ziehen vor they prefer, sie setzen fort they continue, die Unterhaltung conversation.

Die Abreise (ap'rie-zə) DEPARTURE.

Ja indeed, zeitig early, erst only, warten (auf) wait (for), frühstücken breakfast, schon already, vor einer halbe Stunde half an hour ago.

Remark 55: Translate the adverb *ago* by the preposition vor, as: a month ago vor einem Monat; two weeks ago vor zwei Wochen.

Schlafen to sleep, aufstehen to rise, der Koffer trunk, der Bahnhof railway station, fort gone, der Fall case, der Wagen carriage, holen to fetch, holen laſſen to send for, dankbar grateful, die Sache the object, unterbringen to find a place for, der Hausdiener hotel porter, das Gepäck baggage, der Kleiderſchrank ward-robe, ſuchen (nach'ſehen) to seek (look for), finden to find, weg fahren drive off, bekommen to receive, to get, der Kutſcher coachman, die Fahrt the drive, der Tarif tariff, jeder every, das Stück piece, alſo therefore, bezahlen to pay, behalten keep, das Trinkgeld gratuity (fee), das Gepäck abgeben (or aufgeben laſſen) to cause to be delivered (i. e. to have the baggage checked), die Fahrkarte löſen to buy the ticket, der Schalter ticket-window, der Beamte ticket-agent, (Beamter is any government employé—the railways in Germany belong to the government) wiegen to weigh. ungefähr about, das Übergewicht over-weight, excess-luggage, der Gepäckſchein baggage-check, der Warteſaal waiting-room, ein'ſteigen get aboard.

Übung, page 82 : deswegen therefore, eben just, bei at, die Vor'bereitung the preparation, fertig ready, unterdeſſen meanwhile, endlich finally, begeben ſich betake themselves (i. e. they go), ſobald as soon as.

Page 83 : beſchäftigt occupied, melden to announce, ſofort immediately, zuletzt at last, zu Fuß gehen to walk.

Remark 55 : The English *to get something done, to have something done by somebody else,* is rendered in German by laſſen and the infinitive, as : I have the porter carry the baggage ich laſſe den Hausdiener das Gepäck tragen ; ich laſſe mir einen Rock machen I am getting a coat made for me ; ich laſſe das Gepäck abgeben I am having the baggage checked.

Die Ankunft. ARRIVAL.

Sich nähern to approach, der Turm tower, die Reisedecke rug, die Handtasche bag, in Ordnung bringen to put in order, die Droschke cab, besorgen to procure, sich umsehen nach to look around for, halten to stop, aus'steigen alight, der Gepäckträger railroad porter, rufen to call, nach'sehen to look (to find out), die Fahrtaxe tariff, betragen amount to, nötig necessary, sonst otherwise, fordern to demand, die Etage floor (story), wir möchten we should like, darf ich may I, hinaufsteigen to ascend, in Augenschein nehmen to inspect, gefallen to please, to suit, führen to lead, der Hof court-yard, frei free, nach vorn toward the front, gelegen ist is situated, ziemlich gut pretty well, kosten to cost, herauf'tragen to carry up, der Speisesaal dining room, brauchen nur need only, die Treppe stairs, hinab'steigen descend, der Oberkellner headwaiter, ein'treten step in, die Speisekarte bill of fare, das Spiegelei poached egg, der Führer the guide, Befehlen to order, etwas some, doch yes indeed, Kellner, zahlen! waiter, we wish to pay; was macht unser Abendbrot how much is our supper?; gezahlt paid, besorgt settled, besichtigen inspect, da since, kennen to be acquainted, Führer guide, gewiß certain.

Übung : verneinend negatively, Rücksitz backseat, verlangen ask for, hinaus'sieht looks out to, erreichen to reach wenden an turn to (accost), ehe before, mieten to hire, in Bezug auf with regard to, eine Mahlzeit ein'nehmen to take a meal, was es zu essen giebt what there is to eat, gespeist eaten, Fremde strangers.

Ein Spaziergang (PROMENADE) durch Berlin.

Prächtig splendid, solch such. Tiergarten name of a park in Berlin, die Menschenmenge crowd, die Equipage carriage.

der Reiter rider, das Thor gate, hindurch through it, der Platz square, das Schaufenster shop window, die Auslage display, die Hutform hat shape, Galanteriewaaren=Geschäft fancy-goods business, der Regenschirm the umbrella, vergoldet gilded, der Griff handle, vorziehen prefer, elfenbeinern ivory, die Modistin milliner, stehen bleiben stop, neu'an'gekommeu newly arrived, bewundern admire, einen Augenblick a moment, das Juwel (yoo-vail') jewel, die Brosche brooch, bemerken notice, der Handschuhladen glove-store, begleiten accompany, brauchen need, neu new, der Commis (komeé) salesman, dienen serve, der Glace=Handschuh (glassay') kid glove, farbige colored ones, teuer expensive, billig cheap, die Sorte kind, ein'wickeln wrap up, die Kasse the cashier's window, danke verbindlichst much obliged, der Gang passage, führen to lead, manche many a one, belebte Straße lively, (bustling) street, verkehrreichste Straße most frequented street, die Residenz city wherein the King resides, das Gebäude building, die Vereinigten Staaten (fer-ien'igtn shtahtn) the United States, drüben on the other side, der Gasthof hotel.

Übung, page 89 : Wie bringen sie den Nachmittag zu how do they spend the afternoon, der Laden the store, aus= gestellt exhibited, Schmucksachen jewelry, der Zustand condi- tion, state, an'reden to address, to accost, betreten to enter, schließlich finally.

Spazeirgang (continued).

Wieder again, das Bauwerk building, structure, die Ecke corner, die Kirche church, königlich royal, das Schauspielhaus play house, daneben next to it, die Querstraße cross street, Friedrich der Große Frederick the Great, der Stil style, bauen to build, das Opernhaus opera house, ringsum round-about, die Anzahl number, die Sehens=würdigkeit object of interest, der Palast palace, schräg diagonal, gegenüber opposite, die Universität' university, die Wache guard-house, das Zeughaus arsenal, der Kronprinz crown prince, das Stand=bild monument, die Kolossal'statue colossal statue, zurück back, die Brücke bridge, überschreiten go across, das Schloß palace, wenden turn, gelangen arrive, der Lustgarten pleasure-garden, das Bronze=Standbild bronze statue, die Amazone amazon, der Löwen=kämpfer lion fighter, der Durst thirst, der Hunger hunger, die Terrasse terrace, Platz nehmen to take a seat, das Innere inside, interior, das Lokal place, heiß hot, das Kleingeld the change, vielleicht perhaps, die Banknote (der Schein) bill, wechseln to change, gewiß certainly, müde tired, eben just, vorüber past, die Börse bourse, der Säulengang colon-nade, die Sammlung collection, das Gemälde picture, der Künstler artist, ist ähnlich resembles, das Kasta.ien wäldchen chestnut grove, die Haupt=wache principal guard house, der Soldat' soldier, der Weg way, die Säule column, die Sieges=säule the column of victory, die Stadtbahn city railway, vorderste first, der Hintergrund background, die Chaussee (shossay') driveway, der Parkteich park pond, die Insel isle, die elegante Welt high society, zoologisch (tso-olog'ish) zoological, um over, Sie haben recht you are right.

APPENDIX.

DECLENSION.

Singular.

	masc.	fem.	neut.
nom.	{ der große Tisch) { ein großer Tisch)	die große Thüre	{ das große Buch) { ein großes Buch)
gen.	des großen Tisches	der großen Thüre	des großen Buches
dat.	dem großen Tisch(e)	der großen Thüre	dem großen Buch(e)
acc.	den großen Tisch	die große Thüre	{ das große Buch { ein großes Buch

Plural.

nom.	die großen Tische,	Thüren,	Bücher.	The 3 genders of articles and adjectives are alike in the plural.
gen.	der großen Tische,	Thüren,	Bücher.	
dat.	den großen Tischen,	Thüren,	Büchern.	
acc.	die großen Tische,	Thüren,	Bücher.	

Remarks on the declension of Adjectives: The pronominal adjectives (dieser, jener, welcher, jeder, aller) are declined like the definite article. If an attributive adjective is not preceded by an article or pronominal adj. it takes itself the article ending, as: guter Wein, gutes Wasser. Ein, kein and the possessive pronouns (mein, Ihr, etc.) have also the same ending as the definite article, except in the nom. masc. and nom. acc. neut., when they (and the succeeding adj.) have the forms specially mentioned above with ein. If no noun or adj. follows ein, kein, mein, Ihr, etc., they take the article ending even in these excepted cases, as : Wo ist mein Hut ? Meiner ist hier. Haben Sie ein Buch ? Ich habe eins.

Remarks on the declension of Nouns; singular: The e in the genitive ending es and in the dative is elided whenever euphony requires it. Most of the masculine nouns in e and a few other masculines take an n in all the oblique cases, as : Nom. der Knabe (the boy), gen. des Knaben, dat. dem Knaben, acc. den Knaben.

Plural: the masc. just mentioned have their plural in n (die Knaben), other masculines take an e (die Tische, Hüte, etc.), a few take er (die Männer). Masc. and neut. ending in el, er, en in the singular do not take any plural ending as also the neuters in e, chen, lein (sing. der Löffel, der Lehrer, das Fenster, das Gebäude, das Fräulein—plur. die Löffel, die Lehrer, die Fenster, etc.) Of other neuters some take er some e ; feminines take mostly n but some monosyllables take e.

Many masculines and neuters take the Umlaut *in the plural.*

Irregular plurals : Augen eyes, Ohren ears, Enden ends, Mütter mothers, Töchter daughters.

USE OF THE CASES.

The subject of all verbs and the predicate after sein (to be) and werden (to become) is in the nominative : der Mann geht. Ich bin der Lehrer, Er wird ein Kaufmann (merchant).

The English possessive and often the preposition *of* are rendered by the genitive: the man's hat der Hut des Mannes; the cover of the table die Decke des Tisches; the lock of the door das Schloß der (fem.) Thüre.

The dative is the indirect object of the verb, often expressed in English by *to* or *for:* Ich gebe dem Mann ein Buch (to the man). Er macht dem Knaben einen Rock (he makes a coat for the boy). Was sagen Sie der Dame (to the lady).

It stands often with an adjective: das ist ihm angenehm (that is agreeable to him), es ist Ihnen gesund (it is healthy for you), es ist mir warm (it is warm for me=I feel warm).

It also denotes the person in whose interest or against whom something is done: Essen Sie mir das (eat that for my sake). Nehmen Sie dem Knaben die Uhr (take the watch away from the boy).

The accusative is the direct object: Ich sehe ihn. Er schlägt den Hund (he strikes the dog).

It often is used as an adver, ial expression of place or time: Gehen Sie diesen Weg! Kommen Sie jeden Tag? New York, den 4ten Juli.

Remember that the *dative* must be used with: begegnen (to meet), befehlen (to command), gehorchen (to obey), antworten (to answer), danken (to thank), gefallen (to please), helfen (to help), nützen (to be useful), schaden (to harm); the *accusative* with bitten (to ask=request), fragen (to ask=question).

PREPOSITIONS*

With the genitive : wegen,† während. *With the dative:* mit, nach, bei, seit, von, zu, gegenüber.† *With the accusative:* durch, für, ohne, um, gegen. With the *accusative to express direction* toward a place, with the *dative to express occupation* of a place : an, auf, über, unter, in, neben, hinter, vor, zwischen.

Genitive.

Translation of prepositions : Wegen des Regens on account of the rain, wegen der Kälte on account of the cold, meinetwegen on account of me, for my sake, (Ihret= wegen, seinetwegen, unseretwegen, on account of you, him, us, *or :* for your, his, our sake); während des Sommers during summer, während einer Woche during one week.

Dative.

Mit mir with me ; nach Ihnen after you ; bei gutem Wetter in good weather, bei Tage during day, bei dem Herrn at the gentleman's house ; seit vorigem Jahr since last year, seit zwei Tagen since two days (for two days past) ; von ihm, ihr, mir from him, her, me ; zu dem Kaufmann to the merchant ; dem Theater gegenüber opposite the theatre, gegenüber der Kirche opposite the church.

Accusative.

Durch die Post through the post (mail), durch den Regen through the rain ; für mich for me, ohne Sie without you ; um das Haus around the house, um den Garten around the garden ; gegen ihn, sie, mich against him, her, me.

(For an, auf, über, etc., see the tenth lesson.)

---

*To avoid overburdening the student's memory we have omitted such prepositions as he does not need until farther advanced.

Those marked † may also stand after the noun.

www.ingramcontent.com/pod-product-compliance
Lightning Source LLC
Chambersburg PA
CBHW022041080426
42733CB00007B/925